MW01051829

Social Skills
Learning about Feelings

Mini-Books to Teach Essential Social Skills

Carson Dellosa Education
Greensboro, North Carolina

Credits

Author: Kasandra S. Flora, M.S. CCC-SLP
Illustrations: Pam Thayer, Julie Kinlaw, Erik Huffine, J.J. Rudisill

Key Education®
An imprint of Carson Dellosa Education
PO Box 35665
Greensboro, NC 27425 USA
carsondellosa.com

ISBN 978-1-4838-5694-0
01-335197784

Table of Contents

Introduction

Social skills are important. They are like good manners. Using them properly makes it easier to relate to other people with positive outcomes. Children with age-appropriate social skills can more effectively communicate, make decisions, solve problems, create and maintain successful relationships, and manage their own behavior. A lack of age-appropriate social skills interferes with children's relationships with other children, their teachers, and their family members.

Social skills do not come naturally to all children. But, social skills can be shaped. Social narratives—short stories that focus on specific social skills or desired behaviors—are useful tools to this end. They can be written or modified to meet any specific challenge.

Ideas for Using the Materials in This Book

Making the Mini-Books

This book focuses on tasks that are important in building essential skills. These pages present 13 mini-books that highlight and reinforce common behavior expectations. The illustrations are simple and printed in black and white so that children can color them. This interactive component helps children make the mini-books "their own" books.

The story pages are perforated and can be reproduced (two-sided) or assembled as single copies. Some children can cut apart and assemble the pages themselves, then staple the pages together on the left side of the books. (Check that the pages are in the correct order and help children if needed.) You may also choose to bind the books by using a hole punch and yarn or small metal rings.

Once the books are assembled, have children read their completed social narratives aloud. If a child cannot read independently, read the lines to the child. Following the first reading, have children "sign" their title pages and color the illustrations with crayons or markers. Reread the stories as needed. Over time, the narratives will become more familiar.

Repetition

New behaviors become more deeply ingrained each time they are practiced, so it is important to encourage children to read and reread their social narratives (aloud to another person). A goal chart is printed on the back page of each story to help children keep track of their progress toward a goal of reading the social story 10 times. The book concludes with award certificates for achievement and effort.

In This Book

Each mini-book in this book focuses on an important developmental social skill. They can be used in any order and as frequently as needed.

These social narratives are written in simple language so that they can be easily understood and assimilated. We hope they will prove to be an invaluable tool in shaping children's behavior.

I Feel Happy

by _____

It makes me feel happy when I play with my friend.

(3)

(2) Today I feel happy.
I have a big smile on my face.

- -

(4) I feel happy when I eat ice cream.

6

I feel happy when I play with my puppy.

Feeling happy makes me smile and laugh.
It feels good to be happy!

6

I feel happy when I swing at the park.

I will work on meeting
my goal - 10 ✔'s!

Make a ✔ each time you read your story.

I Feel Sad

by _____

I feel sad when my friend does not want to play with me.

(3)

2 Today I feel sad.
My mouth is frowning. My eyes are crying.
And, my stomach does not feel good.

4 I feel sad when my mom leaves me at school.

If I forget my toy at my friend's house, I feel sad and I might cry.

- -

When I feel sad, I can use my words and say, "I feel sad."
When people know I feel sad, they can help me.

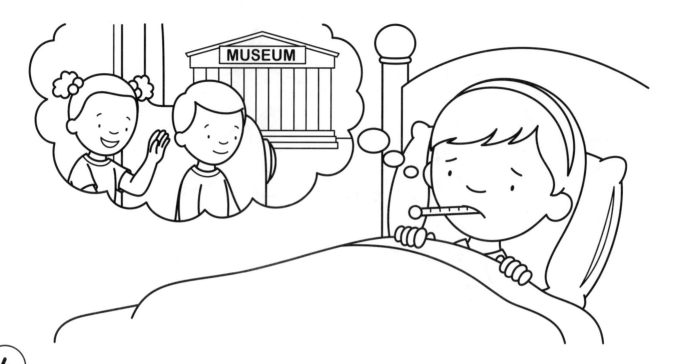

⑥ If I was sick and could not go on the field trip, I would feel sad.

I will work on meeting
my goal - 10 ✔'s!

Make a ✔ each time you read your story.

My Friend Feels Sad

by _____

I want to help my friend feel better.
I can walk over to my friend and say, "What is wrong?"

(3)

(2) My friend looks sad. Her mouth is frowning.
Her eyes are crying. And, she is sitting all alone.

(4) My friend might say to me, "Go away and leave me alone."
Then, I should walk away and tell my teacher.

My friend might say, "No one will play with me."
I can say, "I will play with you."
That will make my friend feel happy.

(5)

If I grab my friend's red crayon, it might make her cry.
She will feel sad.

(7)

15

6 My friend and I are coloring at the same table.
She is using the red crayon.
I want to use the red crayon.

- -

8 My friend feels sad because I took her crayon.
I will give her the red crayon and say, "I am sorry."

16

If my friend falls down, she might cry.
I can be a good friend and help her get up.

9

Everyone feels sad sometimes.
When friends feel sad, they might frown or cry.
I can help a sad friend feel better.

11

(10) My friend and I play games.
If my friend loses, she might be sad.
I can say, "Good game! Would you like to play again?"

- -

I will work on meeting
my goal - 10 ✔'s!

Make a ✔ each time you read your story.

I Feel Angry

by _____

I want to play my video game, but my friend does not.
That makes me angry.
I want to stomp my feet and scream, but that is not OK.

3

(2) I feel angry.
I want to stomp my feet, yell, and make an angry face.
It is better for me to use my words when I feel angry.

(4) I will be a good friend and say in a calm voice, "You pick a game.
We can play my video game later."
My friend will say, "OK."

My teacher might say, "No, it is not time to go outside."
I want to push my chair over and make an angry face.
That is not OK.

(5)

Everyone feels angry sometimes.
I can use my words in a calm voice to tell someone I feel angry.
I can also take a deep breath and count to 10.

(7)

(6) I will be a good student.
I will take a deep breath and count to 10.
I will listen to my teacher and wait to go outside.

- -

I will work on meeting
my goal - 10 ✔'s!

Make a ✔ each time you read your story.

Hitting and Pushing

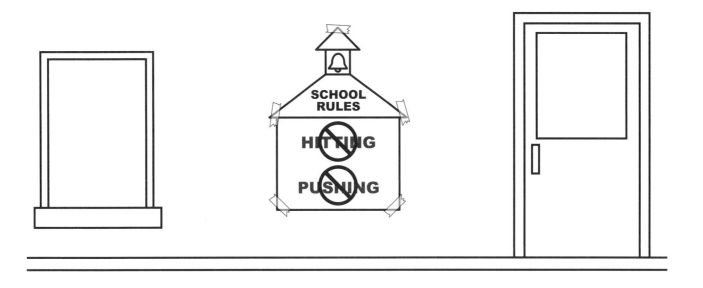

by _____

When I feel angry, I cannot hit other people.
I cannot push or kick other people.
These are school rules.

(3)

Sometimes I get angry at my friends or my teacher.
It is OK to feel angry.
Everyone feels angry sometimes.

(2)

- -

When I feel angry, I can make good choices.
I can choose to follow the rules.

(4)

When I feel angry, I can walk away.
Then, I can relax and calm down in my special way.

(5)

When I make good choices about my angry feelings,
I feel good about myself and my good choices.
And, so do my friends and teachers!

(7)

(6) I can listen to music or read a book.
I can count to 10.
I can take five deep breaths.

- -

I will work on meeting
my goal - 10 ✔'s!

Make a ✔ each time you read your story.

26

© Carson Dellosa • KE-804115

My Friend Feels Angry

by _____

I want my friend to calm down.
I can ask her, "What is wrong?"

(3)

(2) My friend looks angry.
Her arms are crossed. She is stomping her feet.
She is making an angry face, and she is screaming.

(4) My friend might yell at me.
If she yells at me, I should walk away.

My friend is angry because he broke his favorite toy.
I can say, "Do you want to play with my toy?"

(5)

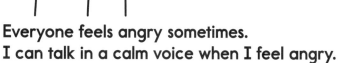

Everyone feels angry sometimes.
I can talk in a calm voice when I feel angry.
I can walk away from my friend when he feels angry.

(7)

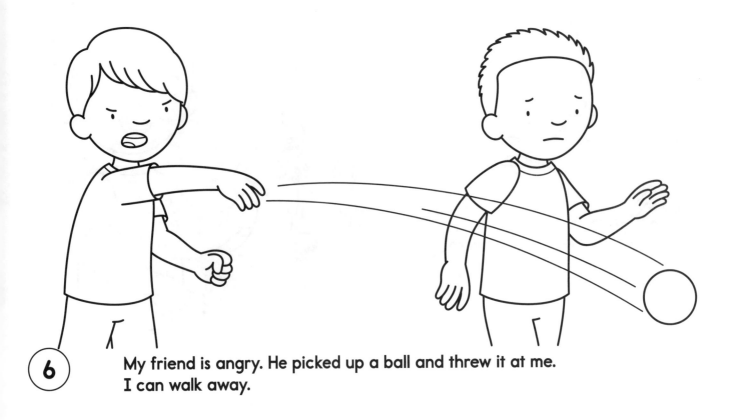

6 My friend is angry. He picked up a ball and threw it at me.
I can walk away.

- -

I will work on meeting
my goal - 10 ✔'s!

Make a ✔ each time you read your story.

30

I Feel Scared

by _____

My friend jumped out at me and yelled, "Boo!"
It scared me. I jumped back and covered my face.

(3)

 Sometimes, I feel scared.
When I am scared, I might cover my face or shiver or hide.

My dad and I heard loud sirens on our drive.
Loud sirens scare me.
Dad said, "Cover your ears. The sirens will be gone soon."

4

I am scared of the dark. I hide under my blankets.
Mom put a night-light in my room.
Now, it is not too dark. I am not scared anymore.

(5)

Everyone feels scared sometimes.
I can use my words and tell people when I feel scared.
Then, they can help me.

(7)

(6) I am scared of spiders.
But, my mom and I can read books about spiders.
Spiders can be interesting. Spiders are not always scary.

I will work on meeting
my goal - 10 ✔'s!

Make a ✔ each time you read your story.

34

I Feel Shy

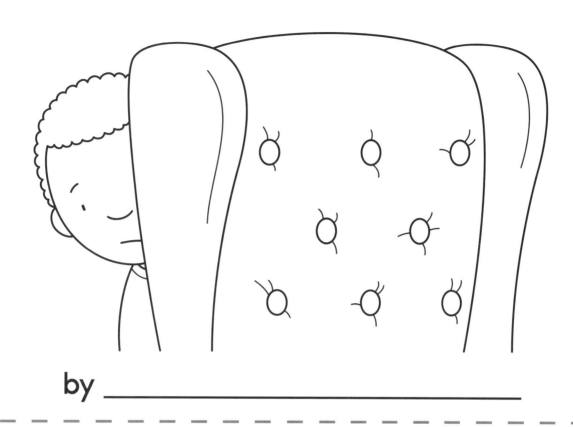

by _____

I feel shy when I meet new people.

(3)

(2) Sometimes I feel shy.
When I feel shy, I look down at the floor.
I do not want to talk to people.

WELCOME STUDENTS

(4) I feel shy on the first day of school.

I feel shy in places where there are lots of people.

(5)

Everyone feels shy sometimes.
It is OK to feel shy.
I can smile and look at people's eyes.

(7)

6

I feel shy when I have to talk in class.

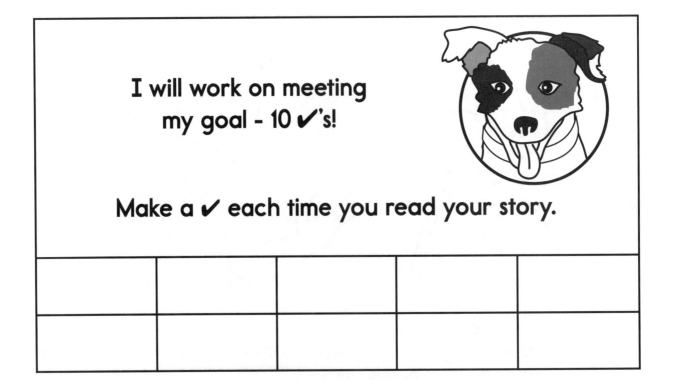

I will work on meeting
my goal - 10 ✔'s!

Make a ✔ each time you read your story.

I Feel Worried

by _____

I feel worried when I go to the dentist's office.
But, the dentist is nice and will give me a treat.

(3)

2 I feel worried. My hands are sweaty.
My heart is beating fast. My tummy feels icky.

Ms. Smith

I feel worried when my teacher is not at school.
My class will have a substitute teacher.
But, my teacher will come back to school soon.

Ms. Smith

I feel worried when I forget to bring my homework to school.

(5)

Everyone feels worried sometimes.
I can tell someone when I feel worried.
Talking about my worries can help them go away.

(7)

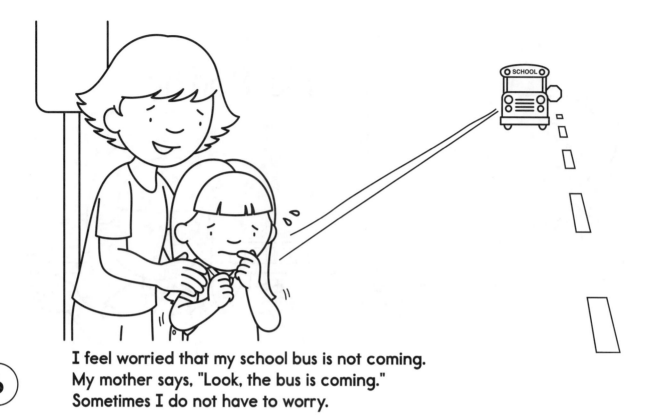

I feel worried that my school bus is not coming.
My mother says, "Look, the bus is coming."
Sometimes I do not have to worry.

(6)

I will work on meeting
my goal - 10 ✔'s!

Make a ✔ each time you read your story.

42

When I Do Not Feel Good

by _____

...hen I do not feel good, it could mean that I am getting sick.
...o not like to be sick.

(3)

Sometimes I do not feel good.
Sometimes my tummy or my head hurts.
Sometimes I have a sore throat or cough a lot.

(2)

When I do not feel good, I should talk to an adult about it.

(4)

I can say to an adult, "I do not feel good. I think I might be sick."

(5)

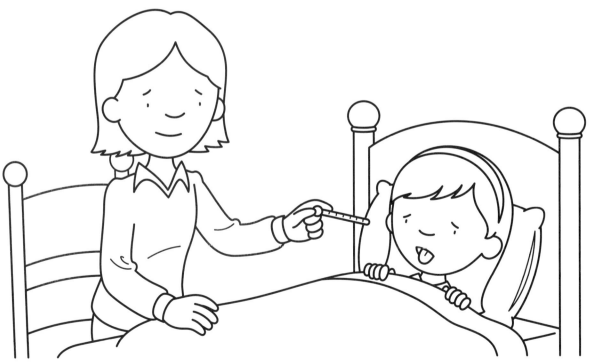

When I do not feel good, an adult can help me.
I will feel better when I get help.

(7)

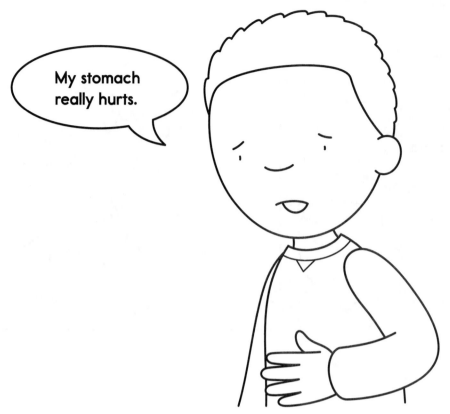

My stomach really hurts.

(6) **Then I will tell the adult what hurts or does not feel good.**

- -

I will work on meeting my goal - 10 ✔'s!

Make a ✔ each time you read your story.

Hugging

by _____

It is OK to hug the people in my family.
I like to hug the people in my family.

(3)

2 Sometimes I feel like hugging.
Hugs feel good.
Hugs are a way to show love.

4 But, it is not OK to hug people at school.
School is not the best place for hugging.

52

I do not hug my friends without asking first.
I do not hug my teachers without asking first.

High Five!

I can give high fives to my teachers and friends.
I can shake hands with my teachers and friends.
These are good ways of touching at school.

(6) I will remember to respect the personal space of my teachers and friends at school.

I will work on meeting
my goal - 10 ✔'s!

Make a ✔ each time you read your story.

I Have Many Feelings

by _____

When I feel sad, my mouth frowns and my eyes might cry.
My stomach might not feel good.

(3)

When I feel happy, I have a big smile on my face.
Something that makes me happy is _____.
I will draw it on the poster.

2

- -

When I feel sad, I can use my words and say, "I feel sad."
When people know I feel sad, they can help me.
Something that makes me feel sad is _____.

4

When I feel angry, I can use my words and tell someone in a calm voice.
I can also take a deep breath and count to ten.

(5)

Sometimes I feel shy.
I look down and I do not want to talk to people.
I will try to smile and look at people's eyes.

(7)

6 Sometimes, I feel scared.
I can use my words and tell people when I feel scared.
_____ makes me feel scared.

- -

8 When I feel worried, my hands may get sweaty.
Talking about worries can help them go away.
Something that worries me is _____.

A happy surprise is when something happens that I do not expect—and I like it!
A happy surprise I would like is _____.

I can feel happy, sad, angry, scared, shy, worried, and surprised.
It is okay to have all these feelings.

59

(10) I might not like it if a friend jumps out and yells, "Surprise!"
I can say, "Please don't yell 'Surprise!' at me."

- -

I will work on meeting
my goal - 10 ✔'s!

Make a ✔ each time you read your story.

Feeling Good!

_____

Name

feels good about learning about emotions.

_____

Signed

_____

Date

A Little Birdie Told Me!

_____
Name

has learned a lot about emotions.

_____
Signed

_____
Date

© Carson Dellosa • KE-804115

_____

by_____

- -

_____

_____

_____

_____

_____

_____

- -

I will work on meeting
my goal - 10 ✔'s!

Make a ✔ each time you read your story.

64